Migi Serrell

The Art of Arranging Flowers

GOLDEN QUILL PRESS
Manchester Center, Vermont
Publishers Since 1902

Golden Quill Press
Manchester Center, Vermont

Library of Congress Catalog Number 96-79054

I.S.B.N. 0-8233-0511-2

Printed in the United States of America

The Art of Arranging Flowers

Water Colors by:

Donna Lewis Parisi

TABLE OF CONTENTS

CHAPTER I

How It All Began

$\mathcal{A}$rranging flowers has had a profound influence on my life and it has been on my mind for the past few years to share my love affair with flowers and the arranging of them with you. I have been teaching and arranging flowers for about 45 years.

In the early years, before I had any idea of what an arrangement was, my mother, Meta Noble, was "fixing" flowers in vases. I would like to establish the important part she played in developing in me the desire to excel in this most creative form of artistry.

Without any formal training, she put together, with a great sense of color and style, one beautiful bouquet after another, all of her flowers coming from her gardens on Round Hill Road in Greenwich, Connecticut.

Mother was primarily a horticulturist and grower. Her formal garden was a delight, a subtle blending of color, form and texture. It was enclosed by a brick wall and guarded by a pair of handsome wrought iron gates from England, two steps down from the terrace level. A small semi-circular pool was on the south face of the whitewashed brick house with a lion's head splashing water from its mouth. It served as the apex for the garden from which the various beds took their design *(see drawing)*. The four center beds were edged with English boxwood, clipped low. In the spring, two of these beds were carpeted with blue forget-me-nots (myosotis) which served as ground cover for early tulips in peach/copper tones. The other two center beds were filled with roses in shades of pink and coral, well pruned and kept low.

On the south or back wall, as well as on each side of the center beds, perennials of all kinds and colors bloomed throughout the summer. I especially recall the tall, stately spires of the King Arthur delphiniums in the brightest of blues, a fabulous background for the large white auratum "madonna" lilies. Under this majestic collection blue ageratum, colorful spires of salvia and pansies, were among other annuals.

Formal Garden.

Many different types of foliage plants were planted throughout, lending a subtle contrast. Iris, astilbe, peonies, as well as heliotrope, were included in most of the larger beds. A pair of flowering almond trees were placed at the south end of the garden where steps led up into the apple orchard. In the early spring these fluffy white blossoms blew in the wind, joining with apple blossoms. Magic indeed!

This was the spring and summer palate of Mother's formal garden. There were other smaller gardens throughout the grounds, but the rock garden was my favorite. It had an almost fairylike quality about it due to its placement, down below a gentle slope, hidden from sight, with a tiny pool fed by a small waterfall hidden among the rocks. Dwarf hemlocks, Japanese cyprus, and compact azaleas rose above underplantings of herbs and native wildflowers. It was peaceful there, full of shadows and the sound of water. The overall design was exceptionally skillful, not in any way contrived.

Beyond a broad expanse of lawn, sloping to the east, Mother planted a thousand or more daffodils, sent to her by her brother-in-law, a famous hybridizer of bulbs in Oregon. The large King Alfred variety were predominately displayed at the edge of the woods. Many other early spring bulbs were planted deep into the woods. These bulbs still bloom there, an everlasting tribute to Mother's talent for creating beauty wherever she could.

As if this wasn't enough, there was a cutting garden below the main house and separated from it by two 100-foot rows of espaliered pear trees, still alive today but showing their age. Part of this area was devoted to vegetables, part to small fruits. The main portion was filled with all the old-fashioned annuals: cosmos, zinnias, salvia, dahlias and the like. Needless to say, a major watering system existed, the source of which was an artesian well, supplying some 60 gallons per minute. That is still the sole source of water on the property.

Is it any wonder that all of this garden bounty found its way into the home and into my Mother's hands? When I think back to recall her arrangements, done without any formal instruction, where she placed them and, most important, the quality of containers she used, it was this enormous talent to which I was exposed on a daily basis.

A word here about the main house which is still "alive" today. It was designed by Phelps Barnum, built in 1930 and is a beautiful example of the Georgian period, whitewashed brick, on what was then 25 acres of farm land. A well, the only source of water for the farm, remains in place today at the top of the drive.

On the east side of the house there is a flagstone terrace which runs the length of the house and overlooks the woods. During the summer there were six tubs of standard lantana or fuschia, depending on their state of perfection. These standards were wintered over in the greenhouse and brought up to the terrace when the weather turned balmy.

Groupings of unique outdoor furniture were placed here and there. I remember well the ceramic backgammon table of cream and blue tile, set up under the old apple tree at the south end near the pair of beautiful English gates I spoke of previously. Beds of lily of the valley carpeted the foundation planting, under a wonderful variety of shrubs. One wonders where to go these days to find that scope of material.

Indoors, in a small room off the main hallway, Mother conditioned the flowers in a deep sink, where plenty of shelves held the eclectic group of her containers, called vases back then.

The most outstanding arrangements were always placed against the white paneled wall under the stairwell. In the summer there would be the blue delphs from the formal garden, combined with the madonna lilies, heliotrope, trailing fuschia and the great gray-blue leaves of the Hosta Glauca. It was one of my favorites and had a great influence on my future. The arrangement itself was fairly tall with classic lines and placed in a lovely white Lalique container, set on an antique wig stand. This spot always reflected the seasons.

In the fall, branches of copper beech with dahlias of rust and wine colors; at Christmas a wire plant stand would be filled with shades of rose and pink poinsettias grown in the greenhouse, and in early spring, freesia, narcissi and dianthus were grouped together on the wire plant stand.

Arrangements for the dining table were a constant source of fun or glamour. Holidays, birthdays, any cause for celebration would bring out her creative muse. Each had a theme; each had special accessories suited to the occasion. When the party was over, all these accessories were packed away in separate boxes and labeled. Shortly after her death, I came upon these treasures and have used them many times in my lectures with great success.

After her death in 1956, I requested and received all of her flower-related items. They have since become the basis of what is a unique collection of containers representing classic lines and colors which blend with flowers rather than compete with them.

After I joined Hortulus in 1945, I was encouraged to exhibit in some local shows which were, at that time, simple and quite unlike the shows which we know today. As I recovered from frequent attacks of stage fright, I began to experiment with different styles of arranging, sometimes going far afield, but always pursuing my idea of beauty. An arrangement of living plant material in its purest form is one of the greatest challenges facing arrangers today; to be creative yet remain within the bounds of good taste.

The following chapters contain almost everything that I have learned over the years. Some step-by-step procedures; some philosophy; drawings and watercolors of different arrangements (some more successful than others!); and, in general, the background and development of the art of flower arranging. It would be gratifying for me to think that this personal view into the world of flowers and foliage might inspire some and encourage others to succeed in this joyous field.

*Summertime arrangement by
my mother, Meta Noble.*

CHAPTER II

A Brief History of Flower Arranging

Flowers have been part of our culture for many centuries and appeared throughout European countries from the sixteenth and seventeenth centuries, as seen in the tapestries and paintings of that time.

It is from the Japanese, however, that we gain most of what we know and practice today. This tiny and sophisticated island of Japan has been pursuing the art of "ikebana," as it is known, for as long as there has been plant material in their gardens. Perhaps one could consider this art as part of their religious beliefs, practiced with restraint and creativity.

Centuries of study have led to purity of design. From no other source have we gained as much as from these highly cultured people who taught us how to dramatize flowers in their various stages of development; to use branches and foliage and enhance their natural growth patterns. Their sensitivity to color, line and form has given us much to ponder. It is from this school that we have learned restraint as well as pure line.

The English loved their flowers and introduced many new and interesting varieties for their gardens. Only those plants that grew where they were not wanted were considered weeds. The arrangements were, and still are, rich in color and texture...full, lavish bouquets which we so admire today. Our present stage of arranging includes this lushness of material which we call, and rightly so, a mass or line mass. These large bouquets were found in the great manor halls and churches in Europe, reflected in tapestries and the great paintings of the Dutch and Flemish schools.

The evolution of our present day arrangements are based on the teachings of both the Japanese and the Europeans but have been simplified for our lifestyle. With a more casual approach, we arrange flowers quickly, as opposed to the Japanese who will spend many hours contemplating a single blossom.

Here in the U.S., we arrange with a lighter heart and for enjoyment, exploring and redefining as we go. We must not ignore the contribution to this art of arranging made by the Impressionist school of painters whose use of color and form have given us yet another direction to follow. The latter part of this century has seen a dramatic change in our approach to arranging. "Creativity" began to assume great importance. Innovative designs, where flowers take a less important role, are called free style and free form, also from the Japanese, as well as abstract design. The latter has caught the attention of our most courageous arrangers. It seems to take the form of sculpture, where plant material is minimal and loses all its natural growth characteristics. Where this particular style will lead us remains to be seen.

CHAPTER III

How To Succeed

*S*ome of us are born with the talent to arrange things, even in our daily lives. Then there are those that just never seem to get it all together. Don't despair! It is to the latter that I offer my help in the world of flower arranging. The others only need restraint! There is a great deal of pleasure to be found exploring the many ways to use plant material (flowers, foliage, branches, etc.) and arranging them in a pleasing manner. The more you handle the material, the more skillful you become. With practice comes confidence and a great deal of satisfaction. Part of the charm lies in the fact that it is a constantly changing medium, as no two stems are ever alike. One never gets bored.

Not everyone achieves success in the beginning, as it takes a fair amount of experience to gain confidence and be successful. Let's qualify "success." Is it a blue sticker at a show?Is it arranging flowers at your church (not easy), or sending a simple bouquet to a friend ? Whichever you choose, remember, if you have pride in your work, you will succeed!

After a certain amount of time and practice you may want to enter the competitive world...an altogether different game. Reading a schedule, understanding the challenges, preparing the material, knowing the rules, are all necessary to a rewarding outcome *(see Chapter X)*.

My advice to the beginner is to attend a few workshops with an experienced exhibitor, one who knows the pitfalls facing the novice. It may be easier on the nerves to enter your first show with a friend who thinks along the same lines as you do. But, after many years of competitive arranging, I advise you to begin to develop your own style and go your own way.

CHAPTER IV

Gathering and
Conditioning Material

This chapter is critical to the
lasting quality of flowers and foliage.

Gathering material for your arrangement is half the fun, provided you know pretty much what it is you need to achieve that special effect. Nature has provided us with an extraordinary variety of shapes, colors, and sizes, each piece with its own design. Everywhere, in all seasons, nature has set before you an extraordinary collection of her specialties: flowers, foliage, branches, mosses, fungi and succulents, all awaiting your selection.

Florists today have many more varieties to choose from compared to a few years ago. A visit to one or more, whether you are in the market to buy or just looking, is a trip around the world.

Conditioning this material before arranging it is the one step that can make or break your heart. Proper conditioning will give the material the best chance of survival in a normal environment. The environment at a show is not normal and takes a bit of understanding.

Here are some safeguards:

1. Always strip off all foliage from stems that will be under water. Any leaves left on will decay under water and shorten the life of the arrangement.

2. There are different treatments for different types of material. In general, all stems should be cut on the diagonal as this allows more water to enter the stem as opposed to a square cut. A cut above or below a joint on the stem opens the way. A small

detail but a good one. Now, place the freshly cut stems into containers with plenty of lukewarm water as soon as possible.

3. When arranging, always make it a habit of recutting all stems regardless of when you have gathered them; from the florist; your garden or wherever. This guarantees an immediate source of water. Flowers also last longer if, after a day or two, the stems are recut and the water refreshed.

4. A package of Floral-Life (or a similar product) added to one gallon of water will definitely prolong freshness.

5. Loosely place the material in tall containers made especially for this purpose and store in a cool, dark place overnight, but not more than 24 hours without refreshing the water and re-cutting the stems. Don't crowd the flowers.

After you have become familiar with this procedure, there will be times when your best laid plans go awry. You will have to experiment a bit...know your material...what it does under certain conditions. Many of the failures reflect poor conditioning or lack of understanding of the needs of the material. The following list gives you advance warning of what to expect with certain flowers and foliage.

1. Tulips can and do change their shape and height while being conditioned. They are very sensitive to light and heat. Some seem to grow overnight, becoming quite perky looking, but will get top-heavy and droop sadly after time in an arrangement. Using them in a show can be risky as the heat and intense light in a niche will provoke them. If you must revive them for any reason, try putting them in very hot water for an hour or so with a copper penny submerged in the water. The hot water treatment may be used in many instances, provided you are not trying to revive dead material. It is worth a try in any case.

2. Roses can be testy, especially those from the florists, because of shipping and handling before they are sold to you. Some won't open at all; some will burst forth and drop their petals. To give them all a good chance, cut the stems on a sharp diagonal, remove all the thorns that will be under water and proceed as usual, giving them 24 hours in deep water. Once they are established, they are quite safe anywhere. Remember: they open gradually and change shape.

3. All woody stems such as stock, lilac, larkspur, etc. and branches should have their stems crushed with a hammer or the like for about 2- 3 inches at the bottom. Some will do well if you take a sharp knife and split the stem 2-3 inches up from the bottom. Lilacs from your yard may resent being used in an arrangement! Remove all foliage from the branch except the small leaves around the blossom. Try hot water overnight in a cool place. Even that is no guarantee. Some branches will respond while others from the same source will not...a mystery which occurs often in the plant world.

4. Some varieties of plants exude a white sap, such as Oriental poppies and the euphorbia family. These stems should be cut off square and burned with a flame to seal in the sap. I use a candle to do this.

5. The foliage of tender plants and those with fleshy veins, i.e., begonias, calla lilies, etc., do best when floated in warm water overnight. Prick the veins here and there with a sharp needle to allow water to enter the leaf more easily.

6. Stems like the calla lily or amaryllis will split and roll up after cutting. Bind the ends with floral tape before using.

While the treatments outlined above sound time-consuming, they are well worth the effort. <u>Remember...strip, cut and immerse</u>.

CHAPTER V

Mechanics:
Keeping Stems In Place

No book on arranging flowers would be complete without a chapter about mechanics, a rather pedantic subject, but one that makes arranging easier, if not foolproof. Consider the carpenter who has at his fingertips all of the tools necessary to complete his job. To the arranger, these are tools to make arranging easier as well as successful. I have a little tackbox which I used in the stable while grooming my horses. It has several compartments and a handle. Today it is filled with many of the things that I have found useful during the course of a career with flowers. I take it with me whenever I lecture or exhibit in a show. A lot of the items lie at the bottom; some are "just in case. But I would not change the mess for any newer method. The list below is a compilation of most needed items. From here on, you are on your own.

Pinholders

These come in various sizes and shapes. They should be heavy and loaded with sharp needles. Some come fixed into a bowl, handy for those containers that don't hold water, i.e., driftwood. The Japanese make the best ones. Remember to keep them clean and free of debris.

Mortite

A caulking compound that can be found in most hardware stores. It is the best product for keeping pinholders in place. It will not set up and become hard like the green plastic sold by your florist. It can be removed easily and doesn't damage the surface of a container. To apply, make sure the surface of the container is DRY. After opening the box, transfer the mortite to a plastic airtight bag to keep it soft.

Twistems

Easy to use. They are nothing more than green, paper-covered wire and do a good job of holding several stems together. They are sold in various lengths at many florists.

Tapes

All kinds should be kept on hand. Floral tape is a lightweight material, pale green, and will adhere to itself. Green cotton-covered wire is used mostly for topiary work but handy in some cases when invisible mending is needed. The dark green, heavy tape which comes on a roll is sticky on one side and I use it to tape down oasis in shallow containers. All are readily available.

Oasis

The primary answer to keeping stems in place. It is a lightweight pale green brick of porous material. It can be cut to size dry or wet. Most important is the process of soaking it BEFORE you use it in a container. It must be completely wet. I put the whole brick into a deep bowl, weight it down with a stone and leave it for at least 10 minutes so all of the brick is wet, inside and out. If not, stems will go down into dry areas, not the idea here. I never reuse it if it has holes left in it from previous arrangements. There is an alternative to oasis for use in tall containers. It requires a bit of patience. The white "peanuts" that come in packages make fine holding material in opaque containers. Fill the container about two-thirds full with these peanuts and add water to the halfway mark. The trick here is to keep them submerged. As the stems are placed in them, they will stay down and keep the stems in place very well. They are clean and reusable. Remember to <u>fill</u> the container with water after you finish arranging.

Pruning Shears and Sharp Scissors

A must. They should be heavy duty and kept sharp. Wire cutters are handy and keep you from ruining the shears. Add a sharp knife and you will have just about all you need.

My favorite "must haves" include green garden stakes to elevate material, test tubes of various sizes, hairpins, dressmaker pins, a box of paraffin used to mend cracked containers, and candles to seal some stems after being cut. As you can imagine, my tackbox looks like a trash bin, but it gives me a feeling of being on top of all problems. When arranging, try to keep the mechanics to a minimum. They should never show.

CHAPTER VI

Containers or Vases

Why is it so difficult to find pleasing, flower-related containers? Those that compliment an arrangement rather than compete with it? I think it is because we tend to look for a container only when we need a special one.

I have a fairly large collection, some that I have yet to use. All of them are user-friendly. One of the reasons for my extensive collection is the fact that when I lecture I like to use several different containers, letting my audience know why they should have more than one from which to choose. Different styles of arrangements require different containers, needless to say.

I am a compulsive collector and look everywhere: tag sales, antique shops, flea markets. Hey, you never know! I used to pass up some wonderful pieces because there was no immediate need. Then I would remember a certain piece months after, and wish I had had the foresight to buy it. I don't hesitate anymore and that is why I have such an eclectic collection on my shelves. My idea of a perfect container is one that has distinction, does not compete with the material you place in it, and gives the owner pleasure even without flowers.

There are many different types of containers. Dutch, French, early American, wonderful old Japanese porcelains, contemporary pieces, garden urns (one of my favorites), driftwood, museum reproductions, art deco glass, Volkmars (rare) and baskets.

It all depends on your needs and taste. Owning a few of these will give you a good start. Period pieces are available from time to time and since many shows include period arrangements in their schedules, it is a good idea to have a few in your collection.

Keep in mind that they <u>must</u> hold water. It is also a plus if they relate in color to plant material. You will soon develop the knack of finding containers at auctions, tag sales or junk shops.

For the contemporary style of the 90s, there are those gifted enough to make their own. If you are one of those, get out the tools along with copper, Lucite, clay, whatever it takes, and more power to you!

An added joy in owning a large collection is making them available to others.

CHAPTER VII

Distinguishing Features of an Arrangement

Following are a few guidelines that you should be familiar with when entering a show. They pertain to recognizing the various types of arrangements which are included in flower show schedules.

The basic requirements for each design are those which have been established through the years and are recognized by Garden Club of America judges. Exhibitors who are experienced arrangers will often "embroider" a style. By that I mean give it their own "flair." This can be overdone. Exhibitors who develop a certain style can be recognized by the judges and this can become tedious. Beware of locking into a certain manner of arranging that gives you away.

While I am on the subject of "sameness," I will go a step further and caution against using an award winning container, yours or someone else's, before a reasonable time has elapsed. Even then, the arrangement must be done with a "new look." And, of course, never copy!

Period Arrangements

The only challenge here is to adhere to the period required in the schedule. Some research is required as to style, color, and material of the period and of course an appropriate container.

Line Arrangements

A simplified explanation of this type would be one that clearly follows the dominant characteristics of the plant material used, i.e. removing all unnecessary "fuzz." There are twelve different lines to choose from! A certain amount of talent is required to execute each arrangement with flair.

Hogarth

Horizontal

Vertical

Crescent

Asymetric

Pyramid

Line Mass

This is similar in some respects to the clean, line arrangement, but now you embellish the line with more plant material, keeping within the limits established by your chosen line. It is a bit more subtle and gracious, lending itself to weddings, parties and church.

Line Mass

A soft and elegant line.

Class:*Pacific Coast.*
Made up of drift wood, Cyprus branches pruned and trimmed.
First Prize.

Mass Arrangement

Almost self-explanatory. A glorious bouquet of many varieties of flowers arranged so that the individual shapes and colors "shine" through. Size is not necessarily the main idea, rather one where the material seems to float in space with color coordination a prime factor. Many of these exhibited today seem far too heavy and tight, losing the individual flowers for an overall static feeling.

Mass

While the preceding types are familiar to most of us, you should be aware of the growing popularity of the contemporary arrangements included in show schedules, such as free style and free form. I will try to explain the characteristics of each.

Freestyle

A spontaneous expression of creativity. The accent here is on creativity. Using all your background and experience with proper techniques and mechanics, you create an innovative design, a design which is purely the work of the arranger. Plant material may be "rearranged" as long as it enhances the design. NO artificial treatment may be used. The container plays an important part here, as it is considered a major contributor to the design. A freestyle arrangement is best

Freestyle

exhibited by itself, with no constricting space to confuse the design. It is an interesting departure from the more familiar arrangements and a very challenging one.

Free Form

This is similar to free style in its creative demands but it takes on a more sculptural outline. It "flows" and has a softer outline. The container enhances the design, even directs it, so that it

Too static. Not free enough.

Freestyle

Birds of Paradise; gilt grapevine,
colored water in pickle jar on copper tray.

Abstract

Construction: globe and painted sticks with
one Bird of Paradise. Painting: "Falling Light."

becomes part and parcel of the arrangement. It is enveloped by the plant material. The words "rhythmic flow" seem to fit the style.

It is best to be completely at home with these styles before entering a class.

If these aren't challenging enough, consider **ABSTRACT**. How arranging ever got to this point will remain a mystery, at least to me. Probably arrangers searching for new fields to conquer! In any case, the requirements completely ignore all the familiar rules of flower arranging. Exhibitors

Free Form

who enter this class are, as the saying goes, in a class by themselves. They are inventive, fearless and have great talent for making their own "containers," a misnomer, since these structures do not have to hold water.

Abstract

To enter an abstract class you should have a clear concept of what the word abstract means. There are many judges who are still confused by the concept. The main thing to keep in mind is that one must present an idea that has no relationship whatsoever to nature as we know it.

I repeat, to understand abstract, you should have a firm grasp on the meaning of the word. The interpretation and the understanding is as confusing as the judging of a class.

Take time and go to the Museum of Modern Art to look at some of the abstract works displayed there. There is one in particular that helped me get a grasp on what made the difference between contemporary art as opposed to abstract. It was a series of small canvases of a cow. The first canvas is indeed a cow in color, shape and background. In the second and third canvases, the familiar shapes are gradually replaced by linear forms. In the last canvas, the cow, as we know it, disappears, replaced by bold color, static forms. Voila! No cow.

Once again, a comprehensive course in abstract art will help clear up some of the difficulties encountered in this type of "arranging"; to forget nature's way and to be prepared to defend yourself against harsh criticism and sometimes less than informed judging.

Oriental

Last, but not to be ignored, are the arrangements in the Oriental manner. Called **IKEBANA**. it is the purest interpretation of nature that can be expressed by arrangers. The ultimate purpose is to place flowers and branches according to their natural growth patterns so that no disrupting elements disturb the individual beauty of each stem. There are symbolic themes involved here that are expressed by the unity of three: Shin (Heaven), Soe (man), and Tai (earth).

Seasonal material tell their story. For example, in the spring a shallow container is filled to the brim with water, but fairly shallow in the fall. Water plays an important role in many of these arrangements when using low, flat containers.

In order to pursue the mystique of Japanese ikebana, one must study the cultural background, preferably with a member of the Japanese school.

CHAPTER VIII

Basic Elements of an Arrangement

In my opinion, a flower arrangement is an art form in three dimensions, incorporating all the basic elements of design, color, form, texture, balance and originality. Look for these elements in all arrangements that you see. The quality of the plant material, the container and its purity of design all contribute to a successful composition.

The terms "arrangement" and "composition" are really one and the same. Arranging is what takes place in order to produce a composition. Webster defines "composition" as the "ordering, arranging or settling of elements into due relationship or position." This is what one does with different shapes, textures and colors, thereby creating an arrangement or composition.

You should be familiar with the various types of arrangements as discussed in Chapter VII, namely the period arrangements, line, line mass, free style, free form, abstract, and the Japanese style called ikebana.

Each of these styles have a definite outline or design. The key word here is DESIGN. The following qualities are what give an arrangement distinction.

Balance and Rhythm

Place the physical outlines of your material in proper relationship, one to another, so that the design flows, making a pleasing unit.

Balance corrected.

Contrast

This is the placement of the material; color, shape, texture, dark against light, shape against form, rough against smooth. All of these qualities are present in the plant material available to you. Use them!

Color

Since color plays such an important part in the design of an arrangement, an in-depth study of color will help you to understand the influence it has on an arrangement and how better to use it. Let me elaborate; there are complementary colors which appear opposite each other on the color wheel, analogous colors which appear on either side of one color, and monochromatic colors which are shades and tones of one color. Black and white are the absence of color *(see Chapter XII)*.

Harmony and Unity

These are present when all the elements are in scale and contribute to the overall design. DIMENSION (so often overlooked) means that one is able to see through, up and down, thereby creating a three-dimensional work of art.

Proportion

Keep the container, as well as the space allotted to the arrangement in mind. Try to recognize "out of proportion." Top-heavy is one; flowers too large for container, another.

Focal Point

A colorful point of interest with a distinct outline, that anchors the design and gives it character.

The finished "product" should be one-and-a-half times the height of the container; one-and-a-half times the width of a low, shallow one. There are exceptions, such as classes where all GCA rules are suspended or the overall look is not pleasing to the eye. Feel free to adjust the proportion to your liking, within reason.

Always try to use an odd number of flowers, keeping them at different levels and on different planes. Buds and light colors seem best on the periphery of the design; in other words, the further away from the axis or center, the lighter the color, the texture and size of the plant material. The darker colors and heavier textures will be best closer to the center of the arrangement.

The placement of material is important in order to achieve dimension, which means being aware of depth, height and width. Using the sides as well as the backs of some flowers or foliage adds interest. Color values, properly placed, also add dimension.

These basic rules exist to help you understand the principles of arranging flowers. When you have reached the point where you follow all of these rules automatically, it may be time to experiment and break a few, or develop a style of your own. Since all of the above end up in one container, it is wise to equip yourself with proper mechanics *(see Chapter V)* and the know-how to use them, so that in the finished product no mechanics show.

Always pursue beauty and distinction.

CHAPTER IX

Here's How!

Now, let's deal with placing your material in a container. Start with an arrangement for your home. Decide what room it will go in and the space it will occupy. I have been known to arrange a bouquet in my garage, bring the finished product into my house and wonder where to put it! Now I have three places that accept my efforts in good grace.

What is the normal procedure? I always start with a container, chosen for the place it will go, followed by the style of arrangement which suits the container. Here's the step-by-step process I use:

My container is 8 inches high and traditional in shape. According to the basic rules, the finished arrangement will be approximately 20 inches high or one-and-a-half times the height of the container.

Next step is to fill the container with material that will stabilize the tallest elements. I use any number of things, but prefer the plastic "peanuts" that come with packaging. They are clean, don't decompose in water, and can be reused. Take care, though, they float. Partially fill the container with water. The peanuts will rise to the top, but persevere. After you place the top or highest elements in their proper position, you will begin to feel the support these peanuts give. There are other alternatives, like oasis cut to shape or chicken wire which I don't use often because it shreds the stems. Remember, if these tall elements are not secure now, they never will be.

Collecting the flowers and foliage should be done at least the day before. This gives you time to condition them properly *(see Chapter IV)*. It seems foolish to go to all the fuss of preparing to arrange the plant material when half of it has wilted.

When selecting your material, keep in mind specific colors as well as shape and texture. You need some foliage and tall elements for height. If the flowers are from your garden or you are buying the material, keep in mind the type of arrangement you wish to do. Florists today sell many flowers by the stem, so there is no need to buy more than you can use. However, it is good practice to always have a few extra pieces of the more important flowers. Don't forget <u>color</u>, <u>shape</u> and <u>texture</u>.

Now that the major decisions have been made, you can start to enjoy the "art of arranging flowers." Get your mechanics together,

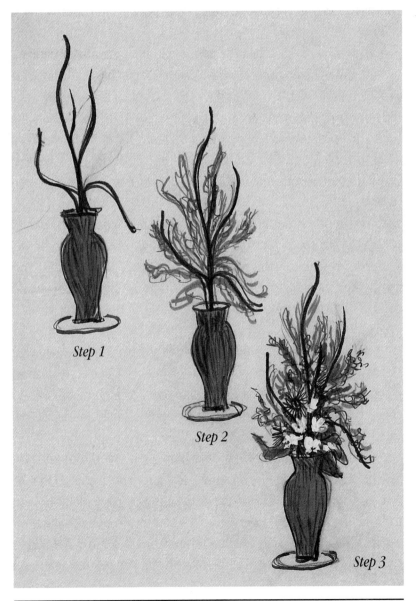

Step 1

Step 2

Step 3

especially a pair of sharp shears. Fill the container with plastic "peanuts" and add water. Now place the container on a turntable, similar to the ones used to decorate cakes, available where cooking supplies are sold. This allows you to turn the arrangement at any time to check on all sides.

Next, establish the main line by placing the tallest pieces firmly in place and over the center of the container. Check to make sure your arrangement is secure at this point, because if it isn't, it never will be!

Now start to embellish the theme with the secondary material, usually the smaller flowers and foliage. Don't forget the interest provided by using the sides or backs of your plant material. Arrange the flowers so that some are at different levels at the sides and at the back. This promotes a feeling of depth, a most important aspect of an arrangement. Avoid a flat look. Lighter colors, the buds and the tapered ends of your material belong at the periphery in this kind of bouquet.

As you proceed, the darker colors and heavier textures should "drift" toward the center. In other words, as you develop the design, you are bringing the whole together toward a focal point. This can be one or two glorious flowers or a group, full of texture and color. This focal point anchors the whole bouquet and gives it pizzazz.

From time to time, stand back to look at what you have achieved so far. Now is the time to make any adjustments. Check the balance. Does it lean backwards or tilt to one side? Use the turntable to check this, filling in or removing the material that clouds the design, eliminating "fuzz."

There will be times when your plans don't work out and you will be tempted to pull everything out and start again. Don't be discouraged. I have been there many times. Just remember, you have handled material, experienced the routine of conditioning flowers, cutting stems, used mechanics and put it all in a container. Nothing was in vain, because the more often you go through these motions, the easier it will be to handle all the elements involved. When you become familiar with the routine you can almost "let your fingers" do the arranging.

Every arrangement that has taken thought and time needs to be cared for: water replenished, stems recut, wilted material removed. Since you've gone through all the elements of arranging, take care of your creation.

There are other more casual approaches to arranging, such as the "bunch" technique which so many of my friends employ with a certain amount of pride. Grab a glass bowl or vase and drop the bunch in it.

If this appeals to you and time is scarce, separate some of the material into about three bunches and put them in separately. You can even cut some of the stems shorter than others so there is a bit of dimension. There is no reason to adopt my classical approach unless you have a hidden desire to create a more sophisticated bouquet.

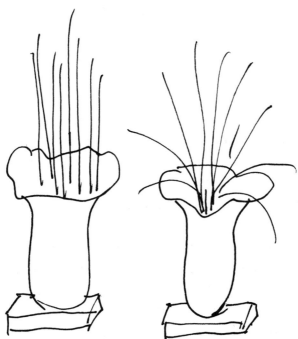

How to deal with a dozen roses.

CHAPTER X

Show Time!

$\mathcal{B}$efore you decide to enter a show, get yourself a copy of the Garden Club of America's Judging Guide for Flower Shows. It contains almost all the important information needed by an exhibitor. You may obtain a copy from the GCA by phoning (212-753-8287) or writing (598 Madison Avenue, New York, NY 10023). If you have read the preceding chapters, as well as the Guide, you should have a fairly good understanding of the challenge involved in entering a show.

A small in-club show is the ideal place for a novice to start. The schedule and the preparation are similar to a major show but the competition and the pressure are shared by friends. Any arrangement done for a competition will bring on certain nervous tension! Here is the place to become accustomed to it and adapt.

As soon as you have made the decision to enter, get a schedule. Select a class that you are comfortable with and one that inspires you. This is the best and only reason to enter any show. Nothing is more trying than arranging for a class that does not inspire you.

As this is your first show, get some advice from some of the more experienced members of your club or from someone who has given you guidance in the past. Sharing ideas and helpful hints will give you more confidence.

Every schedule has a theme. It serves as a guideline for the classes as well as for the exhibitor. It is important to acknowledge the theme, but you can give it your own "twist." Each class is generally a variation on the theme but it is best to stay within the acceptable limits. ALWAYS let good taste be your guide.

Start by choosing a suitable container, one that is easy to work with. Size is important since it has everything to do with the space allotted to the class. The shape and color of the container should reflect the type of arrangement required in the class, i.e., line, mass, abstract, etc., as well as the space involved.

There is a separate section in the schedule for the rules that list the time allowed for arranging, and the time to remove the arrangement. Plant material on the endangered list, as well as important guidelines for each class, are also included. If you have questions, call the flower show chairman or the person who is in charge of the class. Their telephone number is generally included in the schedule.

Keep the arrangement simple and the mechanics at a minimum for your first show. Selecting the material will probably be the most difficult. When that decision has been made, make sure you have enough to "play" with, and that it reflects the mood of the class. Leave enough time to make any changes before "D" day.

Give some thought to the staging: where it is to be placed; the size of that space, and any color values involved with the background. If your exhibit is to be staged in a niche, remember that none of the material may touch any surface; if it's on a pedestal, adhere to the given dimensions. Is the arrangement to be seen from all sides? The schedule will tell you. Proportion is important in every class.

Many in-club shows stage the exhibits on long tables covered with cloth and very little space between exhibits. These tables are usually 29-30 inches from the floor, creating a different problem since the arrangements will be viewed from the top down. If you are in such a class, remember to arrange your entry with this in mind. Dimensions from the floor to eye level are always given in the schedule, as well as the size of the niche and pedestal. When you have questions, don't hesitate to ask.

Most major shows require the arrangement to be done at the show. An in-club show often allows you to bring the finished product. If this is the case, allow enough time to make a few adjustments after you place it in your space. You may do this before the passing committee checks it out for mechanics showing, water leaking, etc., but not after.

Now that you have created, handled living plant material and placed an entry in a show, relax. Look around at your competition, get some ideas for next time. Judges take an insurmountable time to make their decisions. Be patient and try to enjoy the show.

I pretty much follow the same procedure as in the preceding paragraphs for novices, but add in a few extra steps.

Because I have judged many Garden Club of America (GCA) flower shows in the past, and have a copy of the GCA Judging Handbook, I am familiar with most of the content. The handbook is rewritten about every two years or so, so make sure to keep current.

Schedule first. I generally select a show that I enjoy exhibiting in and one that isn't too far afield. Once in awhile I am tempted to go a long distance away, but the process is time-consuming and needs a great deal of planning.

What concerns me most is the overall venue. Is the show considered a major one? Does the theme interest me? Will it be well organized? Last but not least, are the classes of interest to me personally? Then I consider the staging. Are there niches, pedestals, tables, etc.? Why am I so picky? Mainly, because I know my limitations and depend on inspiration in order to do my best.

Once I have committed myself to the show and to a specific class, I check the rules which accompany the schedule, the time allowed for arranging and the restrictions imposed on plant material, i.e., endangered plants to avoid, etc., plus the general outline of procedure.

When I have chosen a class, mental gymnastics begin. I envision all possible ways to do an interesting and provocative arrangement within the spirit of the class, but with an individual approach. For me, the container is the most important and before making the final choice, I will have considered at least three or more. I never use one that I have exhibited in before, or borrow one that has ever won a prize.

Once I have made up my mind, the choice of material will depend on the style of arrangement required in the class: Freestyle; Still

Life; Mass; Design to interpret, or Table Setting. These are just a few of the possibilities offered in a schedule.

Choosing the container and the plant material takes me about a week. After the choice has been made, I order enough material to play with, and begin to put the initial design together. I prepare a place to work where whatever I have done can remain undisturbed. All of the mechanics I need are at hand so that I can proceed without interruption. It takes me at least two or three days to get close to my original concept, but there's no guarantee that changes won't be made.

There are times when I have scrapped one whole arrangement, only to begin again. It can be quite discouraging to say the least, but the whole creative process is the main reason that I have entered the show. It is a rewarding experience and should be regarded as such.

When I am satisfied that the arrangement has captured the design that I have envisioned, I take a Polaroid picture of it, study the film and make any adjustments necessary. All the glaring errors of design, balance and proportion are right there before your eyes. Now is the time to make the changes.

I have already taken into consideration the space involved, the lighting source, the background color and the level from which the arrangement will be seen. Now the arrangement is taken apart, stems recut and put in containers of fresh water. Timing is everything. If the material hasn't been properly conditioned, you will find some of it less than show quality. Make sure you have some in reserve. The day of the show I pack up the mechanics needed and put the flowers and foliage in water in a plastic milk crate. My container is wrapped separately. Every piece has been marked with my name and phone number.

A checklist helps put some organization into an already taxed brain! You should have a list of your plant material for the entry desk with the horticultural names as well as the common names. That is about as ready as you can be.

Bronze container.
Pink anthurium, gladiola buds.
N.Y. Flower Show.

Anthurium and Epiphllum
in clear glass.
"Rhythmic and Etherial Beauty"
N.Y. Flower Show.

The actual arranging at the show is probably the most frustrating of all. Standing behind you are those "critics" who have already finished their arrangements while you are just beginning. Show them you have nerves of steel! Go through the same routine you did at home, taking all the time you need. Granted, the whole atmosphere challenges your nerves. But, remember, you have done your best and that is all you can do.

Before you leave your space, make sure that all the debris from around the arrangement has been removed, that it is placed exactly where you want it in the given space and the mechanics and water supply are checked. These are just good housekeeping chores and as a former GCA judge, I can't tell you how many times these small details have made the difference between a blue ribbon or an Honorary Mention. I have often commented on my judge's card, "Too bad the exhibit was carelessly presented."

CHAPTER XI

Church Flowers

No book of mine would be complete without a few guidelines for arranging flowers at church, since this is where the greatest challenges are faced and met. Vanity and temerity are at risk here, for there is no place that I know of where a group of people – the congregation – sit through the service viewing the arrangements and then feel free to comment after the service. No wonder volunteers are always on Sabbatical!

There are several matters to be considered which will make the job of arranging a bit easier.

First, you should be familiar with church protocol. What is allowed in the sanctuary? What colors are used at certain times of year? How are Thanksgiving, Christmas and Easter celebrated? Weddings and funerals are usually arranged through the families involved, many families prefer to have professional florists provide the decor. Attention should be paid to the timing of the event so that the church is open and the sexton alerted.

Memorial flowers are also done with the family's requests taken into consideration. Generally there is a flower fund provided for these occasions. The church office should be able to provide you with the names of those who have requested flowers for a particular Sunday. Quite often flowers used at a wedding can, with permission, remain in place for the Sunday service the following day. If you are responsible for the arrangements for that particular Sunday, check the arrangements to make sure the flowers are fresh enough to last through the next service. If not, minor adjustments may be made.

Many churches use a pair of arrangements on either side of the pulpit or, in some cases, one large bouquet on the communion table in front of the cross. If the latter is the preferred placement, be sure that the arrangement does not exceed the height of the cross.

If you are lucky enough to have a flower room available, there will usually be a choice of several types of containers. Unless there is a specific request, the choice is up to you. If you are not inspired by what is on hand, there is nothing to prevent you from using your own. Know the date of your commitment well in advance so that the flowers can be ordered or picked from your garden and be properly conditioned. If you are buying the material, check on the amount of money you are allowed and always obtain an invoice. Sign it and give it to the office secretary. If you use flowers from your garden, you may put a monetary value on them and take a tax deduction. (I have never done this.)

Except for the winter months, I usually use flowers gathered from my yard: interesting foliage, flowering branches, tall grasses, whatever seems appropriate. Sometimes this type of arrangement is more interesting than the usual florist type. Try to follow the seasons for color and material whenever possible.

Thanksgiving, Christmas, Easter, Mother's Day, etc. all require a bit more thought. Check on how these particular days have been handled in the past.

If there is a flower room, it is yours to arrange in. The necessary mechanics should be available, but don't count on it. Be sure to get the key to the church on Friday as most churches are closed on Saturday.

If I am doing a pair of arrangements on either side of the pulpit, I choose my containers and set them side by side on the flower room counter with ample space between them. The material has been well conditioned at home and I will divide it into two, more or less equal, bundles. I place the tallest elements in both containers, anchoring them well, thereby establishing the main line. I finish one arrangement before starting the second, which will follow along the same lines, making last-minute adjustments to both. I rarely have leftover material and the two arrangements are pretty well matched. Don't fuss if they are not exactly the same.

In my church the parlor table is done by the same person. This is generally a small but interesting bouquet that is placed on the coffee table where everyone gathers after the service. The narthex has a spot for something simple which could be a plant or small collection of greens. On regular Sundays these two arrangements are quite informal, but at times of a special celebration they should reflect the occasion.

When the arrangements are finished, make sure that all doors to the sanctuary are open so you can carry them without interference. If they are to be on the pedestals, place them dead center and make sure that they are finished on all three sides. There should be enough space for the minister to pass them on the way to the pulpit.

Now, clean up the flower room!

Here is a list of material that I use when left to my own discretion: Eucalyptus, copper beech leaves, pampas grasses, pussy willow, bare branches with character, fruit, holly with berries, all types of lilies, berried branches, bittersweet, almost anything that speaks of nature. Most of these have good lasting qualities and can serve as a basic structure for many other kinds of flowers. Remember, keep it simple.

Examples of seasonal church arrangements

Autumn

Spring

One of a pair: Left pedestal.

Church flowers: One of a pair.

CHAPTER XII

Color Study

*B*efore you close the cover on this book, I want you to be aware of the importance color plays in an arrangement. Used with knowledge, it can turn a dull, static bouquet into a work of art.

If you study the relationship between colors and what they do when placed one against another, you will have the key to an exciting dimension in the art of flower arranging. There are simple, informative books on color which explain these relationships.

Briefly, the primary colors are red, blue, yellow and green, referred to as "hues." Each primary color or hue has a value, or its relative lightness or darkness. Further:

- **Shades** of a color are made by adding black.
- **Tones** of a color are made by adding gray.
- **Tints** of a color are made by adding white.
- **Intensity** means brightness of color.
- **Analogous colors** are those found side-by-side on the color wheel.
- **Complementary colors** are those opposite each other on the color wheel.
- **Monochromatic** means the shades and tones of one color.

You will find all of the above in flowers. When you place them together according to the system above you will create some startling results. Once in a while a show will have a class calling for a monochromatic arrangement. This means an arrangement in shades and tones of one color including the container. Be aware that white and/or black is the absence of color.

The study of color is a fascinating one and contributes a great deal to art in any form.

One of a pair: Fruit in an epergne.

Notes

Notes

Notes

Notes

Notes

Notes

Notes

Notes

Notes

Notes